LOLO
The World Traveler

WRITTEN BY BARBARA A. GRIFFIN
ILLUSTRATED BY FAISAL SAIFI

LOLO The World Traveler, Alaska
Copyright © 2020 by Barbara A. Griffin.

For information contact:
heardeaglespress@gmail.com

ISBN: 978-1-7357556-0-1 (paperback)
ISBN: 978-1-7357556-1-8 (hardback)

10 9 8 7 6 5 4 3 2 1

TO OUR BELOVED SISTER, DELORIS. YOU WERE
ALWAYS ADVENTUROUS AND LOVED TO TRAVEL.
MAY THIS BOOK HONOR YOU.

– BG

Hi! My name is Lois, but you can call me LOLO.
This is my dog Bella, and we love to travel.
We live in Georgia with my mom and dad.

Tomorrow, we are going on a vacation
to Alaska, and I'm so excited!
We will be traveling in our **RV**.

Canada and Alaska are **adjacent** to each other.
Canada is in a different country so,
we will need our **passports**.

An **RV** (recreational vehicle) is a van that has a bed and kitchen
that people live in while on vacation.
Adjacent means next to.
A **passport** is a small book that allows us to
travel from country to country.

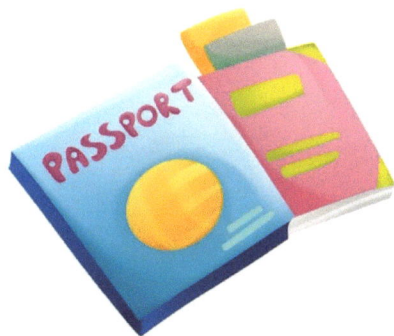

It's time to get on the road!
We want to get an early start to have
more time for fun!

We have a long trip ahead of us.
I have my purse, passport, and Bella,
so I am ready to go.
Are you ready?
Let's go!

From Georgia to Alaska is over 4,300 miles.
That's about 72 hours of driving.
It will take about six days to get there.

We've been traveling for a few hours,
and we are passing through **Atlanta**
on our way to Tennessee.
Goodbye, Georgia!

Alaska, HERE WE COME!!!

Atlanta is the capital of Georgia.
Georgia is known as the "Peach State,"
but it also produces pecans,
peanuts, and Vidalia onions.

Georgia State Capitol

85

We are almost there! We've been
traveling for four days, and we are in **Wisconsin**.
We have two days left before we get to Alaska.

Look at the black and white cows!
Dad! Can we stop for some ice cream?

Very interesting...read this!

Wisconsin is the dairy capital of the
United States and is sometimes called
"America's Dairy land."
It is believed the first sundae
was served in Wisconsin on a Sunday.

Yippee!
We finally made it to Canada
and we are crossing the **border**.
Brrr!
It's getting colder.
I need my coat.
Do you have yours?

A **border** is a dividing line between two countries.

The United States and Canadian Border

Today, we are traveling through
the **Yukon Territory** in Canada.
Tomorrow, we will be in Alaska.
I can't wait!

The mountain **snowcaps** are so pretty.
Wow!
These trees look different
from the trees in Georgia.

Look, A moose!

The Yukon Territory is the northwestern
part of Canada that is wild and
mountainous with very few people.
A **snowcap** is the snow
at the top of a mountain.

Wake up! Wake up! We are here!
We have driven through Canada, and now
we are crossing back into the United States to Alaska.

Look at the grizzly bear family!

Alaska is known as the "Last Frontier"
because of its distance from the other
forty-eight states, its **rugged** landscape, and
frigid climate. Alaska is mostly covered in
permafrost. During the winter, the
temperature can get as low as -40 degrees.

Alaska is the 49th state. **Rugged** means
an uneven or rough surface. **Frigid** means
very cold. **Permafrost** is permanently frozen soil.

After traveling for six days, we finally
made it to **Juneau**, our first vacation stop.

We toured the Mendenhall Glacier.
We hiked up the mountain using **trekking poles**,
went inside ice caves, and paddled canoes
on the lake.

We saw mountain goats, penguins,
bald eagles, and porcupines.

We had so much fun!

Juneau is the capital of Alaska.
Trekking poles are hiking sticks with
handles used to keep you from falling on the snow.

Today, we are on a whale watching tour!
It is so much fun trying to spot a whale.

Did you know?

There are nine different types of whales in Alaska.
Different whale **species** can grow up to
100 feet long and weigh up to 200 **tons**.
Whales can eat up to 1.5 tons of food per day.
Whales feed mostly during the summer months
and live off fat **reserves** during the winter.

Species is a group of living things.
Reserves is stored food.
The most common whales in Alaska
are the orca and the humpback.
Whales mostly eat krill and small schooling fish.

The helicopter tour of the
Matanuska Glacier was so cool!
This glacier is humongous!

Listen to this...

The Matanuska Glacier is 27 miles long and
four miles wide. It is the largest glacier
in the United States that is accessible by car.
A glacier is fallen snow that has been
compressed into a sheet of large, thick ice.

Compressed means that its been squeezed together.
Humongous is a synonym for very big.
One mile is equal to 5,280 feet.
Accessible means able to get to.

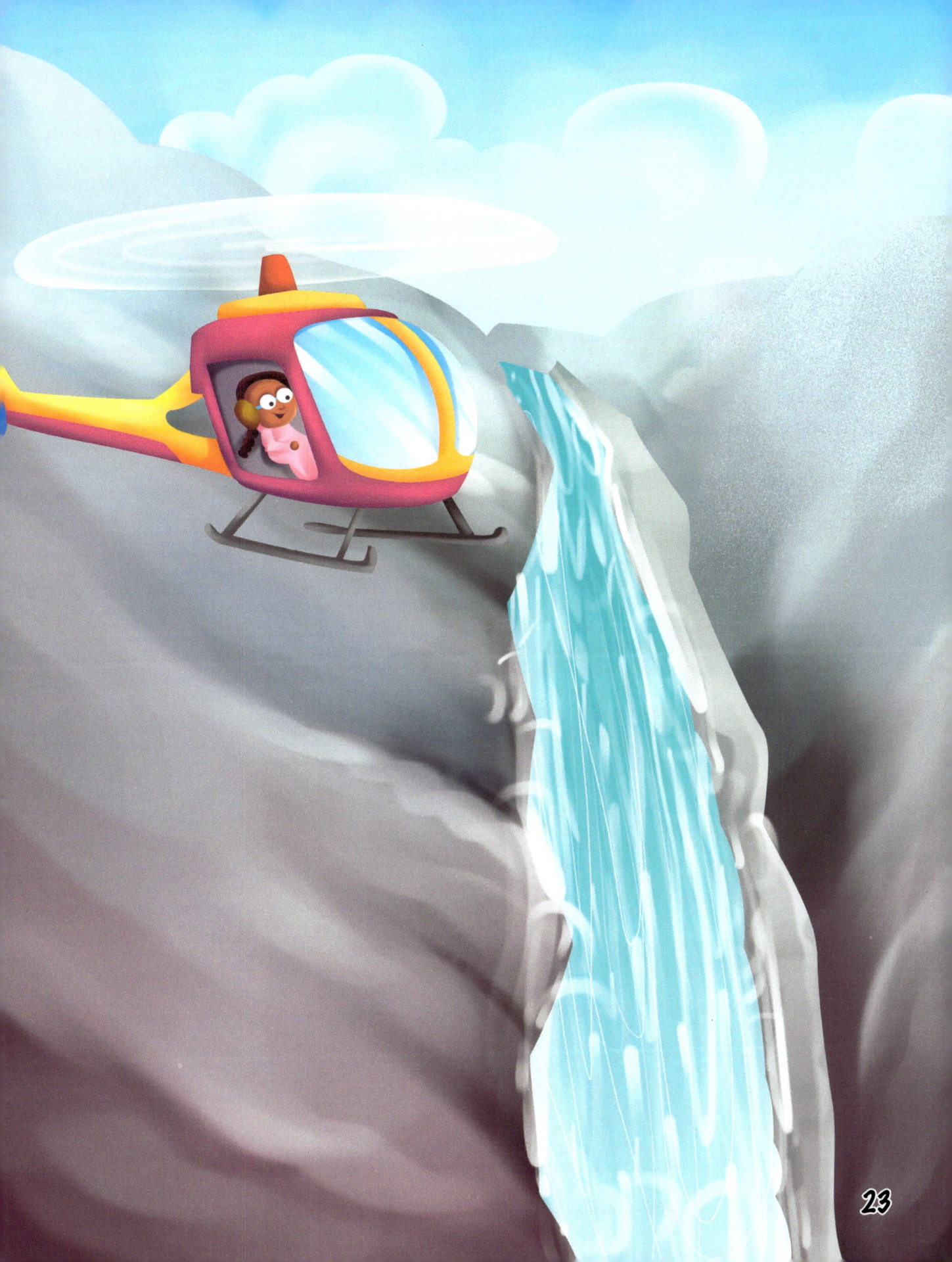

Look!
I'm a **musher**!
We are dogsledding at Norris Glacier.
The **Alaskan huskies** are pulling our sleds.

MOVE OUT OF THE WAY!
This is so much FUN!
Whee!!!

Something good to know...

Many years ago, dogsleds were used for delivering
supplies to communities during **harsh**, cold winters.
Huskies were used to pull the heavy sleds because
of their strength and **endurance**.

A **musher** is the driver of the dogsled.
An **Alaskan husky** is a sled dog that is used to pull sleds.
Harsh means causing physical discomfort.
Endurance means being able to do something that's hard.

Wow! A huge **iceberg**!
So pretty!
I wish I could touch it!

Did you know?

When we see ice bergs, we don't see all of it.
Icebergs are different shapes and sizes.
An **iceberg** is a large chunk of ice that has broken off
a glacier and is floating freely in open water.
Ninety percent of the iceberg is below the
water's surface and ten percent is above.

Icebergs can be as small as ice cubes or as big as
small countries. Just by looking at the
part you can see, it is hard to know the size
of the part under the water that you can't see.

Tonight, we are in Fairbanks to watch the
Northern lights.
We are staying overnight in an **igloo**.

Very interesting...

The **Northern lights** are called the Aurora Polaris
or polar lights. They are natural-colored light
displays that are **visible** in the night sky.
In Alaska, Fairbanks is the best place to see the
Northern lights. Alaska sometimes has long
winter nights and long summer days.
Some places in Alaska can have up to 67 days
a year of darkness. Sometimes, during
the summer, the sun is still out at midnight.

An **igloo** is a house that is built out of snow.
Natural means coming from nature.
Visible means able to be seen.

Now, we are taking a train tour and riding bikes along the countryside. The air smells so fresh.

HOLD ON BELLA!!!

I'm **snowmobiling** in the snow.
This is so exciting!
There are SO MANY fun things to do in Alaska.

A **snowmobile** is a motorized vehicle
used for travel in the snow.

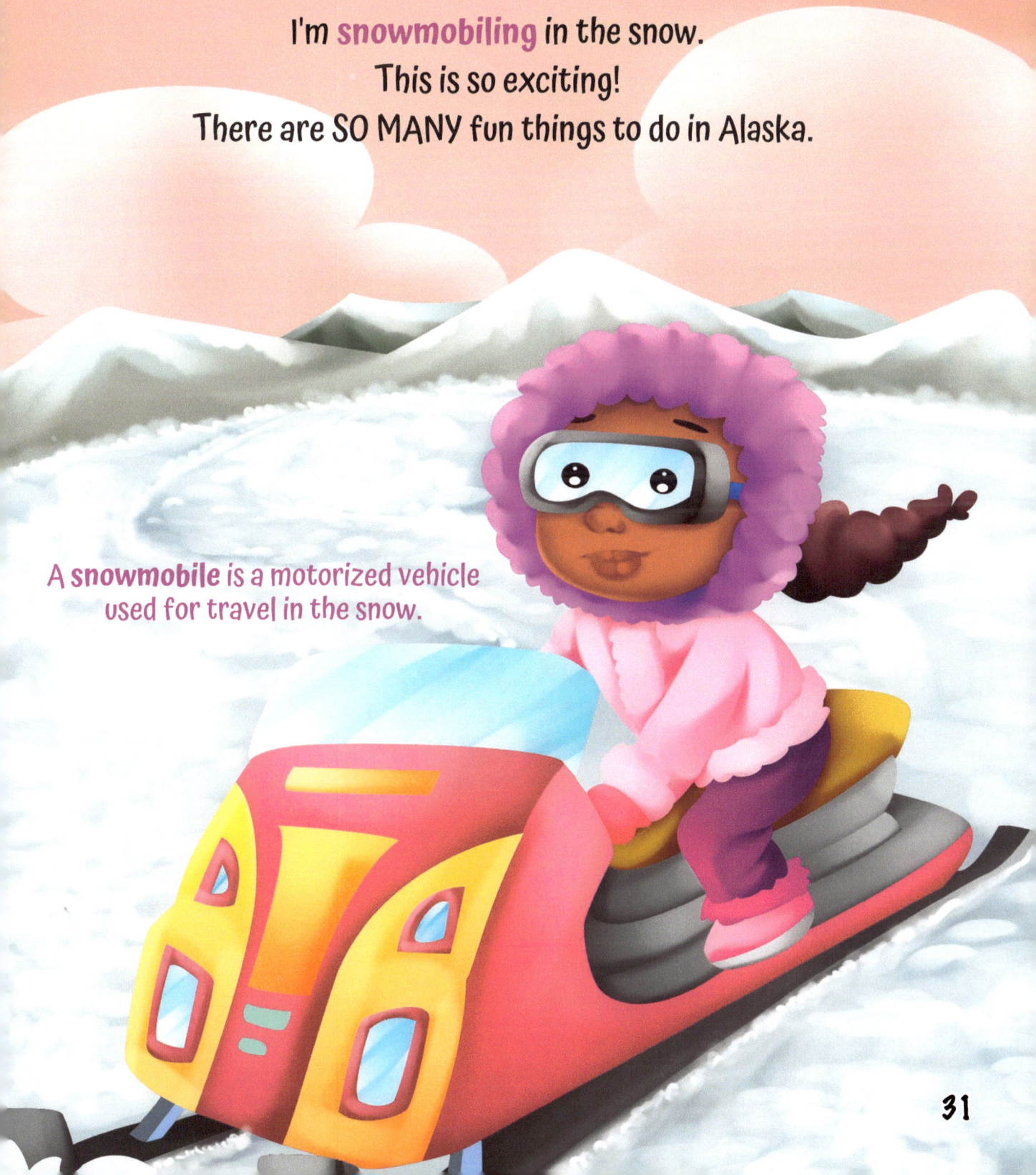

Today, we are **ice fishing**!
We've caught a lot of fish.

There's a polar bear!
He is nearly **camouflaged** in the snow.

Did you know?

Ice fishing is when a hole is cut in the
frozen lake to catch fish.
Ice fishing first started over two thousand
years ago in the United States and Canada.
Camouflaged means to blend in with the
colors around you and hide.

I can't believe I'm standing at **Whale Bone Arch**!
I'm very close to the Arctic Ocean and the North Pole.
So AMAZING!!!

Say what?

Utqiagvik's **Whale Bone Arch** is known as the
"Gateway to the Arctic Ocean." It is pronounced UUT-kee-AH-vik.
Utqiagvik, formerly known as Barrow,
is the northern most city in Alaska.
Utqiagvik has a **population** of about 4,300 people.

A **population** is a whole number of people living in a city or place.
Because of Utqiagvik's **remote** location, groceries are **expensive**.
A gallon of milk and a box of cereal costs about $10 each.
Remote means far away in the distance.
Expensive means it costs a lot of money.

North
Pole

I'm sad our vacation
is over and it's time to go home.

We traveled all over Alaska and
had lots of exciting adventures.
We learned so much and had so much
FUN; I HOPE YOU DID, TOO!

But, GUESS WHAT?

It's time to plan our next
vacation, **and you're coming, too!**

Bibliography

Alaska Shore Excursions. (2020, March 30). https://alaskashoreexcursions.com/

Alaska Trekker. (2020, April 4). Alaska Whales. https://alaskatrekker.com/alaska-wildlife/alaska-whales/

Merriam-Webster. (2020). Merriam-Webster.com dictionary. https://www.merriam-webster.com/dictionary

National Geographic Kids. (2015-2020). U.S. States. https://kids.nationalgeographic.com/explore/states

State of Alaska. (2020, March 30). https://alaska.gov/visitorHome.html

Travel Alaska. (2020, March 30). https://www.travelalaska.com/Destinations/Regions.aspx

9 781735 755601